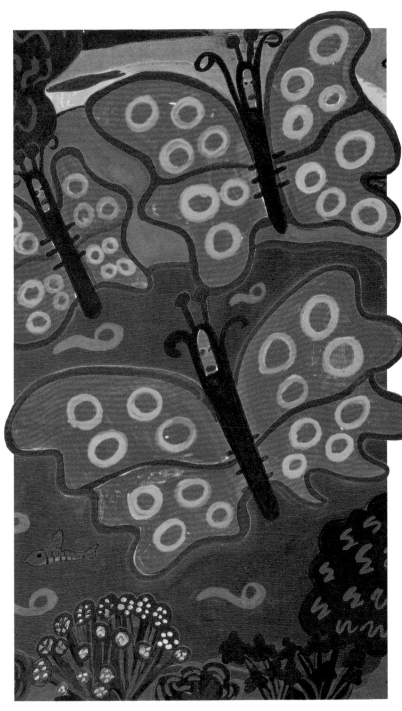

SPRING
A HAIKU STORY

SELECTED BY
GEORGE SHANNON

PAINTINGS BY
MALCAH ZELDIS

GREENWILLOW BOOKS
NEW YORK

For Anne McConnell
—G. S.

For Herbert W. Hemphill, Jr.,
a dear friend and supporter of
artists everwhere
—M. Z.

The full-color paintings were prepared with gouache paints
on paper. The text type is Cloister Open Face BT.

Printed in Singapore by Tien Wah Press
First Edition   10 9 8 7 6 5 4 3 2 1

◆ ◆

LIBRARY OF CONGRESS CATALOGING-IN-PUBLICATION DATA

Shannon, George.
Spring: a haiku story / by George Shannon ;
pictures by Malcah Zeldis.
      p.   cm.
Summary: A collection of haiku verses which describe
the wonders of spring.
ISBN 0-688-13888-8
1. Haiku—Translations into English. 2. Haiku—Illustrations.
3. Spring—Juvenile poetry.   [1. Spring—Poetry.   2. Haiku.
3. Japanese poetry—Collections.]   I. Zeldis, Malcah, ill.
II. Title. PL782.E3S43   1996   895.6'1008—dc20
95-2265   CIP   AC

FOREWORD

Haiku poems have been written in Japan for centuries. Many of the poems included here have been enjoyed for three hundred years. In Japanese, haiku follow the form of three short lines: the first with five syllables, the second with seven, and the third with five. When haiku are translated into English, the number of lines and syllables often has to change, but the essence of the poems remains.

Each haiku poem evokes a moment of "Ah!"—a sensation of seeing something as if for the first time. Each poem is vivid, yet brief, like the experience itself. It may be joyful or sad or a bittersweet blend.

I have arranged these poems to suggest the story of an early spring walk that is filled with "Ahs!," and I am delighted that Malcah Zeldis agreed to illustrate them. Her vibrant paintings are as fresh and immediate as the haiku moments themselves.

—George Shannon

The snow thaws—

And suddenly the whole village

Is full of children!

—ISSA
(translated by Lewis MacKenzie)

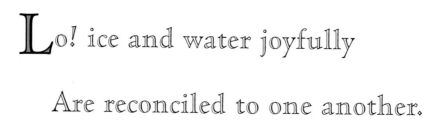

Lo! ice and water joyfully

Are reconciled to one another.

—TEITOKU

(translated by Asatarō Miyamori)

The drake and his wife

Paddling among green

Tufts of grass

Are playing house.

—ISSA

(translated by Peter Beilenson and Harry Behn)

Green frog!

Have you just been

Newly painted?

— RYŪNOSUKE

(translated by R. H. Blyth)

Above the meadow

a skylark, singing, flies high,

high into silence.

—CHIYO
(translated by Harry Behn)

What a splendid day!

No one in all

The village

Doing anything!

—SHIKI

(translated by Peter Beilenson and Harry Behn)

The wild geese fly back to country

After country without a calendar.

—SHUMPA

(translated by Asatarō Miyamori)

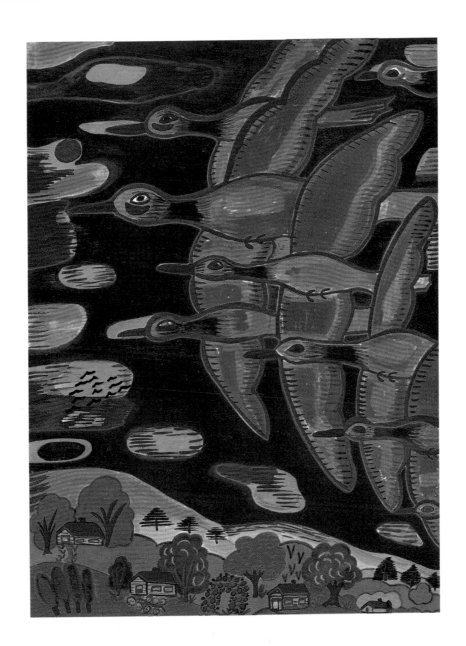

Hear those baby mice

Huddled in their

Nest . . . peeping

To the sparrowlets.

—BASHŌ

(translated by Peter Beilenson)

A willow tickles awake a big dog.

—ISSA
(translated by Hiroaki Sato)

The old pond:

A frog jumps in,——

The sound of the water.

—BASHŌ

(translated by R. H. Blyth)

The first butterfly,

So full of life,—

It's all excitement!

—SHUN'ICHI
(translated by R. H. Blyth)

Going back home

By a different path,—

These violets!

—BAKUSUI

(translated by R. H. Blyth)

Look snail,

Look, O look

At your own shadow!

—ISSA

(translated by R. H. Blyth)

Spring rain:

Everything just grows

More beautiful.

—CHIYO

(translated by R. H. Blyth)

ACKNOWLEDGMENTS

Grateful acknowledgment is made to the following publishers, authors, and translators for permission to include material from their publications:

"The snow thaws" by Kobayashi Issa from *The Autumn Wind: A Selection from the Poems of Issa*, translated and introduced by Lewis MacKenzie. Originally published in 1957 by John Murray Ltd, London. Copyright © 1984 by Kodansha International Ltd. Reprinted by permission. All rights reserved.

"Lo! ice and water" by Matsunaga Teitoku and "The wild geese fly back" by Shimomura Shumpa from *An Anthology of Haiku, Ancient and Modern*, translated and annotated by Asatarō Miyamori. Originally published in 1932 by Maruzen Company, Ltd. Reprinted by Greenwood Press in 1970.

"The drake and his wife" by Kobayashi Issa and "What a splendid day" by Masaoka Shiki from *Haiku Harvest (Japanese Haiku, Series IV)*, translated by Peter Beilenson and Harry Behn. Copyright © 1962 by The Peter Pauper Press.

"Green Frog" by Akutagawa Ryūnosuke and "The First Butterfly" by Taki Shun'ichi from *A History of Haiku in Two Volumes: Volume II, From Issa up to the Present* by R. H. Blyth. Copyright © 1964 by R. H. Blyth. Reprinted by permission of The Hokuseido Press.

"Above the meadow" by Fukuda Chiyo from *More Cricket Songs: Japanese Haiku*, translated by Harry Behn. Copyright © 1971 by Harry Behn. Reprinted by permission of Marian Reiner.

"Hear those baby mice" by Matsuo Bashō from *Cherry-Blossoms: Translations of Poems by Basho, Buson, Issa, Shiki, and Others (Japanese Haiku, Series III)*, translated by Peter Beilenson. Copyright © 1960 by The Peter Pauper Press.

"A willow tickles" by Kobayashi Issa from *From the Country of Eight Islands*, translated by Hiroaki Sato and Burton Watson. Copyright © 1981 by Hiroaki Sato and Burton Watson. Used by permission of Doubleday, a division of Bantam Doubleday Dell Publishing Group, Inc.

"The old pond" by Matsuo Bashō and "Spring rain" by Fukuda Chiyo-ni from *Haiku, Volume II: Spring*, by R. H. Blyth. Copyright © 1950 by R. H. Blyth. Reprinted by permission of The Hokuseido Press.

"Going back home" by Hotta Bakusui and "Look snail" by Kobayashi Issa from *A History of Haiku in Two Volumes: Volume I, From the Beginnings up to Issa*, by R. H. Blyth. Copyright © 1963 by R. H. Blyth. Reprinted by permission of The Hokuseido Press.